No Matter What, God Is There

Stephanie McCuistion

ISBN 979-8-89428-701-0 (paperback)
ISBN 979-8-89428-702-7 (digital)

Christian Faith Publishing
832 Park Avenue
Meadville, PA 16335
www.christianfaithpublishing.com

Printed in the United States of America

To my son, Cody, our beautiful
angel watching over us.

This is a small collection of writings I have done to express things in my life that I have or am going through. I feel that there may be others out there feeling that life is hopeless for them right now, and my hope is to have them read this collection and see that there is hope and that God is always there even when you think you are all alone.

God's Embrace

In the depths of darkness, where shadows
loomed, a child unwanted, I silently bloomed.
But in that solitude, I found solace rare, for
God, my companion, was always there.

When the world turned its back, dismissing
my worth, God's love embraced me, giving me
rebirth. In the tender whispers of the gentle breeze,
I heard his voice, putting my heart at ease.

Through the tears I shed, feeling all alone, God's
presence enveloped me, making me his own.
He held my fragile spirit, fragile and small,
shielding me from the world's bitter downfall.

In the quiet of the night, when fears would arise,
God's comforting hand wiped the tears from my
eyes. He whispered words of love, like a lullaby,
assuring me that in his arms, I would never cry.

Though the world may judge and deem me
unwanted, God's love for me remained, never
daunted. For in his eyes, I was a precious
creation—a testament to his boundless adoration.

Through every trial, every moment of despair, God's
unwavering presence he would always share. He
walked beside me, guiding my every stride, turning
my pain into strength, my wounds into pride.

So though I may have been an unwanted
child, God's love for me was never defiled.
He stayed by my side, through thick and
thin, embracing me as his cherished kin.

His Grace

In moments of sorrow and despair, when life's burdens feel too much to bear, seek solace in the Lord above, his grace and love an endless river of.

Through trials and tribulations, we find a steadfast faith, an unwavering mind. For in the darkest of nights, his light shines bright, guiding us toward hope and respite.

In the storm's fierce winds and crashing waves, God's presence, unyielding, saves. He strengthens our spirits, and our souls ignite, with courage and wisdom in his sight.

Teach our children in this world so wide to trust in him, in whom they confide. For in every challenge and every test, God's glory shines, his love does rest.

So let us stand tall in his embrace, knowing that his mercy and grace will carry us through. With hearts held high in his glory, we'll soar beyond the sky.

May this poem remind you of the enduring strength and love of God, even in tough times.

Christians All the Time

In every step we take, in every word we speak,
let's show the love of Christ, strong and meek.
For outside the church, amid the world's
throng is where our faith truly belongs.

Not just in pews and hymns sung loud, but
in actions kind and heads unbowed.
To treat all as Jesus did, with compassion rare,
with open hearts and minds, ready to care.

For Christianity is not a Sunday guise
but a way of life, a daily prize.
To love our neighbors as ourselves in
this mission, let our hearts delve.

So let's shine brightly, like a beacon true, guided
by Christ's teachings through and through.
For in showing his love both near and far,
we reveal the light of the morning star.

May this poem inspire you to share the love of Christ outside the church walls with everyone you meet, just as he did during his time on earth.

The Broken

In the pews of the church, where souls gather tight,
a longing to connect, to share our inner light. But
often, a barrier stands invisible yet strong. As the
congregation hesitates to know our story long.
For in our brokenness, we bear scars unseen,
stories of pain and struggle, where hope may
have been. But the church, with its facade
of perfection and grace, fears the messy
truths that may darken its sacred space.

They crave published narratives, neatly tied
with a bow, where triumph and joy are the
only tales to show. But life's complexities,
its shadows and its strife, are often deemed
unwelcome, disrupting the holy life.

Yet within each heart, a yearning remains, to be
seen and understood, to break free from chains.
For it is in our vulnerability, our shared humanity,
that true connection blossoms, fostering unity.

So let us challenge the walls that divide and invite
one another to lay our masks aside. For in the
depths of our stories, we find common ground, a
tapestry of experiences, where healing can be found.

May the church be a sanctuary, a place to
be real, where authenticity and compassion
can truly heal. Let us embrace one another
with open hearts and minds, for it is through
our stories that God's love truly shines.

Lost Ones

In the heart of a church family, love abounds
where souls find solace, where hope resounds.
But amid the warmth, a soul stands apart,
haunted by shadows with a guarded heart.

Within these hallowed walls, a tale untold,
a wounded spirit scarred and bold. For
in the depths of past abuse and pain,
fear lingers like a relentless chain.

The church family gathers, arms open wide,
their love embracing, a comforting tide.
Yet this wounded soul hesitates to reveal,
afraid to trust, afraid to truly feel.

But God, in his wisdom, knows the depths within.
He sees the scars, the battles fought, and the sin.
He understands the fear, the need to hide and
gently whispers, "Child, I'm by your side."

God's love is a balm, a healing embrace. With
grace and mercy, he offers solace. He knows
the journey, the struggle to forgive, and in
his presence, this soul can truly live.

The church family, though unaware of the
pain, continues to reach out, their love not
in vain. They offer support, a listening ear,
creating a space where healing draws near.

Yet the wounded soul still fears to let go, afraid
of judgment and of what others may know.
But God's thought is clear: his message divine
in vulnerability, true strength we find.

For within the church family, love can mend
when broken hearts find courage to transcend.
And in the embrace of God's redeeming grace,
the wounded soul finds a sacred space.

So let us pray for the wounded and afraid
that they may find solace, their fears allayed.
May the church family be a beacon of light,
guided by God's love, shining ever bright.

Patience of God

In the darkest hour, when shadows loom, God's presence shines, dispelling gloom. Through trials and tribulations, I find his love and grace, forever kind. When storms assail and hope seems lost, God's hand steadies, no matter the cost.

In the depths of despair, I feel his embrace guiding me gently with unwavering grace. In times of sorrow, when tears freely flow, God's comfort soothes, his peace does bestow.

He carries my burdens and eases my pain, whispering solace like a gentle rain. When doubts consume and fears take hold, God's wisdom unfolds, his truth untold. He grants me strength to face each day, renewing my spirit, lighting my way.

Through life's trials, I've come to see
God's unwavering presence, eternally.

In the worst of times, his love remains a
beacon of hope amid life's strains.

So I'll trust in him, through thick and thin,
knowing his love will always win. For even
in the darkest hours, somehow God's light
shines brightest, guiding me now.

Everyone Matters

Attempting to explain myself, only to be met
with chastisement and a feeling of being in the
wrong, is disheartening. It is important to foster an
environment where open dialogue is encouraged,
allowing for understanding and empathy to flourish.
Let us remember that everyone's perspective is
valuable, and by listening with compassion, we
can bridge the gap between generations and
build stronger relationships within our family.

Wanting to Belong

In the shadows cast by the world's
embrace, I wander lost, a soul displaced.
A sense of not belonging, a constant ache,
alone I stand; my heart does break.

Among the crowds, I feel unseen, a stranger
in a land that's not my dream. Isolated
whispers echo in my mind, yearning for
a place where solace I can find.

But in this solitude, a chance does lie to delve
within, to spread my wings and fly. For in
the depths of my own being, I'll discover
strength, resilience, and meaning.

Though the road is long and the path
unclear, I'll embrace the solitude without
fear. For in this journey, I'll find my way to
a place where belonging will forever stay.

So I'll rise above the feeling of despair,
embrace my uniqueness with love and care.
For in this world, I may feel alone, but within
myself, I'll find a home of my own.

Words

Words hold immense power, and when
spoken without consideration, they can
inflict wounds that may never fully heal.
It's crucial to remember that our words have
the potential to deeply impact others, even
with seemingly insignificant comments.
Before we speak, let's pause, reflect, and
choose our words wisely, always mindful
of the potential harm they may cause.

Unseen

In the shadows, she silently dwells. A
woman unseen, her story untold. Her voice,
a whisper lost in the breeze, is ignored
by those who only seek to seize.

Her presence, a mere convenience to some,
only noticed when they want to overcome.
They come and go with selfish intent,
blinded by the pain her eyes lament.

But God, the witness of her silent cries, sees the hurt
that within her heart lies. He hears the words she
cannot speak and wipes away the tears on her cheek.

In her solitude, she finds solace divine, a
refuge where her spirit can truly shine. For in
the eyes of God, she's cherished and known,
her worth and beauty eternally shown.

Though the world may overlook her grace,
God's love surrounds her in a warm embrace.
He sees her strength, her resilience untold,
and in his presence, her spirit unfolds.

So let her not be defined by other's gaze, for
God's love illuminates her darkest days. In his
sight, she's seen, she's heard, she's known—a
woman of worth, with a spirit that's grown.

Mask or Genuine

In the sacred halls where sermons soar,
where faithful hearts in worship pour, an
age-old question gently blooms: Do church
members care or merely assume?

For when the pews are filled with grace, do
we seek true solace in every face? Or do we
wear masks, a charade to see, in front of
God and others who we pretend to be?

Is the splendor of stained glass a mere facade
while hearts remain unyielding, untouched, and
sad? Are hymns sung with love, transcendent,
and pure? Or are voices raised to simply allure?

When hungry souls crave solace and aid,
do benevolence and kindness pervade? Or
are words of comfort spoken so daintily, a
show for others, for God perfunctory?

Amid the crowded pews, do we truly engage with
the plight of our neighbors, their sorrow, their rage?
Or do we maintain distance, aloof and removed,
bound by our own righteousness, truth unproved?

For the church's hallowed embrace dwells
compassion and mercy, devoid of space. If
hearts fill with love, sincere and vast, the
congregation thrives, making shadows cast.

Let us shed pretense, shed deceit, and rise
above the show, insincere and fleet. For
God, the witness of our innermost strife,
seeks authenticity, a genuine life.

Let genuine care cascade from us all. As
faithful servants, we answer the call to
embody the love, we preach and adore to
show God's compassion forevermore.

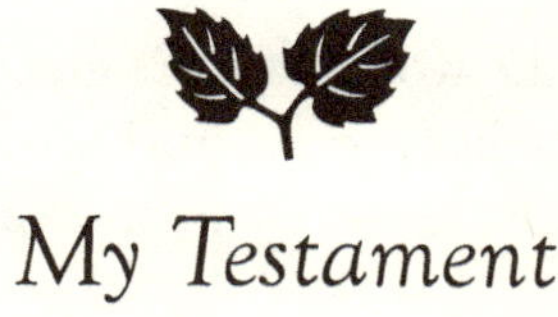

My Testament

In the warmth of a hallowed place, where sacred
words and hymns embrace, I yearn to share my
heartfelt tale of how God's love did never fail.

From the tender age of five, I knew his presence,
near, remained so true. Through trials dark within
my home, his guiding light was never known.

Adopted kin, who caused me pain, in shadows
felt by tears, I'd wane. But in his grace, I found
refuge, a strength that helped me to refuse.

Abuse and hurt, the scars ran deep, yet
God's embrace my soul did keep. He
whispered hope in darkest nights, his
love embraced, mending my plights.

If only I could tell my church how God's love
quelled up pains of a wicked lurch. From tender
years in all my strife, he saved my very gift of life.

But though the words fail, his grace remains in
every breath my heart sustains. For God's presence,
unwavering sure, keeps me anchored, safe, secure.

So I shall worship, give him praise in every step
for all my days. For God has been my rock,
my guide, and in his arms, I'll ever abide.

Let Me Be Me

In a world of expectations, I yearn for release,
to shed the chains of conformity, to find inner
peace. No longer will I bend to fit society's mold,
for my worth lies not in the stories I'm told.

I'm tired of hiding behind this painted grin, with
a smile on my face while turmoil brews within.
They ask, "How are you doing today, my dear?" But
they don't want to hear the truth, it's crystal clear.

They see my facade, the laughter I display,
assuming all is well, that I'm okay. But
beneath this mask, a weariness resides, a
yearning for authenticity, for genuine tides.

I refuse to be defined by others' desires, to
succumb to the pressure, to stifle my fires. I
am more than an illusion, more than just a
role; I long to be real, to regain control.

So, dear world, take heed of this plea I make;
let me be true for my own sake. No more
pretenses, no more empty smiles, I yearn
for connection for truths that beguile.

With courage I declare, enough is enough; I
am more than a facade, more than a bluff. No
longer will I strive to fit within your embrace;
I'll embrace my own self, restore inner grace.

Memories of the Missing

In the midst of the festive cheer, Christmas
dawns, yet solitude is near. Missing two of my
precious boys—one departed, one far from joys.

Oh, how I yearn for their warm embrace,
their laughter, love, and familiar grace.
One's presence is silenced by fate's decree
while the other journeys far from me.

But this sorrow I bear within, aching silence,
hidden by a grin. For no one cares to sit and
hear the depths of pain that I hold dear.

Yet amid the mirth and glee, I'll cherish
memories in whispers free. I'll reminisce
on love that once bloomed, in the hearts
of my dear boys now consumed.

For though the world may fail to see the heaviness
that cares to be. I'll hold their spirits close and
near, embracing their absence, shedding a tear.

So Christmas holds a bittersweet glow, a
reminder of the love we'd come to know.
For my boys, I'll light a candle bright,
guiding them through this lovely night.

Unyielding Spirit

In the quiet stillness, I stand here strong,
listening to every word, right from the throng.
I feel the emotions, the highs and the lows;
there's more to me, more than anyone knows.

Though unspoken, I understand the pain—
the games played, the lies that remain.
It hurts to witness the deceit unfold, yet
presence remains steadfast and bold.

But within my depths, resilience resides,
unyielding spirit, where compassion abides. Know
that I am here, a shelter in the storm, a haven
for truth, where your heart can transform.

Embrace your voice, let it resound; for in unity,
healing can be found. Together we'll rise, stronger
than before, in this journey of life, forevermore.

Stand Together

In a world so vast, where love can unfold, there's
a bond between siblings like pure gold. For
you, my dear children, a poem I shall weave, a
message of unity, and the love you receive.

Spawned from a heavenly realm up above, you
were destined to bring joy, kindness, and love.
Gifts from the divine, with hearts intertwined,
united forever, an unbreakable bind.

In your essence, a reflection of God's grace,
with each other in this lifelong embrace. Never
forget, my children, the importance of kin;
through thick and thin, always let love win.

Banish the anger, let go of pointless fights,
choose understanding, and mend all divides.
No need for whispers or secrets concealed; let
honesty and trust be your eternal shield.

Remember, my darlings, to cherish one another;
in a world full of chaos, be each other's anchor.
Stand tall as siblings, united and strong;
through every storm, you'll always belong.

Take a Chance

In a world that judges quickly, I wish they'd
take a chance to see, the real me beyond my
strife, to know the depths of my life.

I may not make it easy, I admit, a consequence of
the pain I've dealt with, abuse that's haunted me
through the years, leaving scars and hidden tears.

But if only they knew, if they could see the strength
I found, the fight in me, how God's love saved me,
so young and frail, and how his grace prevailed.

Still, I'm often forgotten, it seems, left alone in
my daily stream, even from church and leaders
divine, who turn away, never giving me their time.

I wonder what God would truly feel if he
witnessed these actions, so unreal. Would
he be saddened by their lack of care, by the
way they ignore my burdens to bear?

So I write this poem to plead my case, to
ask for understanding and embrace, to
let people in, to give me a chance, to see
beyond the surface, to join in my dance.

I long for connection, friendship's touch, solace,
and comfort, to mean so much, for someone
to listen, without judgment or lies, to see the
strength in me and wipe away my cries.

So please, give me a chance and don't let me
fade; see the real me beyond the masquerade.
Together we can overcome our past strife and
find solace in each other amid this lonely life.

Connection

In the depths of my heart, a pain resides as
an adult child's love seems to slide. I long
for connection, a bond that's true, but it
hurts when their affection is askew.

Lonely tears fall, for I yearn to be seen, to
know they value me, just like they deem.
But alas, they choose others over my name,
leaving me feeling lost in this painful game.

False words spoken, tales twisted and turned,
my heart breaks as trust slowly burned. *How
can they believe such untruths?* I wonder as my
soul aches from this emotional thunder.

In my disabled state, I carry a heavy load,
physical pain mixes with heartache untold, yet
all I desire is love and understanding to mend
the bond and find joy in withstanding.

Though sadness surrounds me, I will not
despair, for in art's embrace, I find solace there.
Through canvas strokes and words on a page,
I'll express the depths of my pain and rage.

So I turn to creativity, my refuge and guide,
a realm where emotions can truly reside. And
though the wounds may never fully heal,
through art's creation, my heart finds appeal.

God's Always There

In the depths of my sorrow, when I feel so alone,
there's a beacon of hope that guides me back home.
God's presence—unwavering, steadfast, and kind—
is a refuge for my weary soul, a solace I find.

In this world filled with judgment and deceit,
God stands tall, offering love so complete. No
lies or humiliation from this divine source, only
truth, compassion, an unwavering force.

Through life's trials and pain, I find solace
in him, for he understands my struggles
even when life seems grim. His love is
unconditional, unyielding and pure, a love that
heals wounds and makes my heart secure.

In moments of weakness, when sadness
takes hold, I find strength in knowing God's
love never grows cold. With open arms, he

embraces me with care, whispering words of comfort, reminding me he's always there.

So in the darkest moments, I find solace and peace, knowing God's love for me will never cease. He's my refuge, my rock, my guiding light, always present, always true, forever shining bright.

God Always Cares

In my moments of darkness, when struggles
seem too much to bear, I find solace in
knowing that God always cares.
Though I may be poor in wealth, my
spirit is rich with faith, for he provides
in mysterious ways, never late.

Through hardships and pain, his love shines
bright, guiding me through the darkest night.
When loneliness creeps in and sadness fills
my heart, I feel his presence, never apart.

God's divine hand reaches out, lifting me up
high, sending help and hope from the sky.
In times of need, his mercy flows, comforting
me with the grace he bestows.

So I rest in his promise, knowing I am not
alone, for in his care, I have found my home.
Though the road may be tough, I walk it with
grace, for God's love surrounds me in each embrace.

Dear God

Dear God, my eternal guide, in your love, I
always confide. From the age of four, alone and
scared, your presence is a comfort that bared.

In the silence of the night, I felt your
presence, a guiding light. Through
childhood fears and unknown lands, you
held me close with gentle hands.

No judgment from your divine gaze, just
unconditional love that stays. Through
every trial and every test, with your love,
a constant, my heart is at rest.

So thank you, dear God, for being by my side,
for loving me wholly; with you, I confide.
In your love, I find peace and truth, forever
grateful for your unwavering youth.

My Heart Cries

From the moment of my birth unwanted, unloved
here on earth, physically, emotionally torn apart,
and told I was nothing, with a heavy heart.

With bruises hidden, words that sting a young
child with no song to sing, praying not to face
another day, yearning for the pain to fade away.

From one torment to another, the cycle repeats.
Love twisted into anger and deceitful threats
of losing a child. I was fighting for my life,
only to face more struggles and strife.

Cancer's battle, a war within, leaving me
broken beneath my skin. A mere shell of what
once was me lost in a world of misery.

Through it all, God's hand I see steadfast beside me
in times of plea. But where are his other children
today? Why have they turned and walked away?

My surviving children, adults now grown—their
love for me is perhaps not shown. Unable to hear
my silent cries, they ignore the pain behind my eyes.

Every day, in a battle with pain and fear alone,
I shed a silent tear, longing for someone to
understand, to hold my hand, a helping hand.

In solitude, I face my plight, longing for someone
to hold me tight, to listen, to understand
my pain. Why must I suffer in the rain?

God doesn't make mistakes, they say, but in my
story, where do I stay? Alone in the darkness, I
search for light, hoping for peace out of sight.

Did Jesus....?

In a world of sorrow deep, did
Jesus smile and softly weep?
With miracles and tales to tell, did
laughter from his lips compel?

Did he crack jokes with his friends, or
in silence, did his message blend?
Amid the trials and the pain, did
his humor gently rain?

In the modern world, would he find
mirth in the chaos and the birth?
Would his laughter light the way
to a brighter, hopeful day?

May his spirit guide us through, with
humor, grace, and love so true.
In the mystery that remains, let's
seek his joy amid our pains.

Comfort of Others

To make people comfortable and happy,
I must always wear a mask so snappy. But
at least with God, it's not needed, for he
knows what my heart has seeded.

Why can't people be more like him, seeing
beyond the surface and not feeling grim? Let's
strive to see with eyes that truly see, embracing
each other, being who we're meant to be.

Lessons

Though we've had some struggles in the past,

The things you've taught me did surely last.

The hope, love, and patience you always did show.

Through my kids and me, your
teachings continue to grow.

I know my antics were a lot to endure.

Your love and God's were surely the cure.

God's Dream

From above where the heavens gleam, God watches
over his earthly dream—
his children lost in a world of sin, judging, hating,
not looking within.

Pretending to be righteous and true, we forget the
love he wanted to imbue,
acting as Christians only in sight yet missing the
essence of his light.

In sorrow, God sees his children stray, yearning for
them to find their way,
to embrace kindness, compassion, and grace, and to
let go of judgment without a trace.

May his love reach deep into each heart, guiding his
children from worlds apart,
for in understanding and love so true, his children
find peace and joy anew.

God's Design

In God's design, we all are made unique in form and
    outward shade—
different colors, shapes, and faces—yet inside beats a
    heart, a sacred place.

Though diverse in appearance we may be, our souls
    unite in humanity—
love and kindness, a deep connection, a universal
    bond, a shared reflection.

So let us celebrate this divine plan, embrace the dif-
    ferences hand in hand.
For in our essence, we are all one in God's image;
    together we are spun.

Goodbye, My Dearest Friend

In the quiet calm of twilight's embrace, we walk
together in a sacred place. Your loyal heart for-
ever beats with mine in every step, in every sign.

Through fields of gold and skies of blue, I see your
spirit running true. In dreams, you wag your
tail with glee, forever bound just you and me.

Your paws have left their prints in my soul, a bond
unbroken, making me whole.
Though you've crossed the rainbow bridge above,
you'll live forever in my endless love.

Little Ones

In the laughter of little ones, pure and sweet, even
     with the sadness in my past, their joy replete.
God's gift of grandchildren makes life complete, a
     beacon of light, in love's retreat.

Their tiny hands and smiles so bright, a midst my
     pain a comforting light.
Even as parents argue in the night, in grandkids'
     embrace, all feels right.

Blessed are we to watch them grow, to guide them
     with wisdom, love to show.
Despite the trials we've come to know, in their pres-
     ence, our spirits aglow.

In the eyes of our grandkids, love does shine, a bond
     eternal, divine, and fine.
God's grace in every laugh and whine, in their inno-
     cence, a love so divine.

Made the Same

In the eyes of God, we are all the same, no disabilities, worth, or fame. A heart beats within each chest, equal in His eyes, we are blessed.

Some Christians may think their heart is right, but do they truly love with all their might? Do they treat all with equal care, or do they separate, unaware?

Let kindness and compassion guide our way, seeing beyond differences, come what may. For in the end, it's what's inside, that truly matters, with love as our guide.

Following Jesus

In Jesus's steps, I long to tread, but obstacles
loom in my way like shadows of dread.
People and trials try to lead me astray, yet
I hold onto faith, come what may.

Amid the chaos and noise, I hear a
whisper, a still, small voice.
Guiding me with love and grace, in
Jesus's footsteps, I find my place.

Though the road is rough and steep, his
light shines bright, my soul to keep.
With each hurdle, I grow strong,
for in his love, I truly belong.

Embrace the Fear

In the heart of man, a primal fear, of the unknown, drawing near. It's human nature to dread the end, yet in heaven's arms, we'll ascend.

Embrace the fear, let it pass through, for in death, life begins anew. It's only human to feel this way, but in eternity, joy will stay.

Heaven's Light

In the shadows of fear, I find solace in the sky, for in heaven above, my soul will fly. No more pain to bear, no tears to cry, just endless skies where dreams can never die.

In death's embrace, I'll find relief, no longer burdened by my earthly grief. In breath, to walk, to run free, in the arms of angels, forever to be.

Remember that your words have power to lift your spirits in your darkest hour. In heaven's light, you'll find your way, where pain and sorrow fade away.

Unspoken

In shadows of my silence, my emotions quietly dwell, their weight upon my shoulders, a story I can't tell, a child within my heart, still seeking to be heard, but words unspoken, lost in the echo of a world.

Your gentle barbs like arrows, pierce my tender soul, invisible wounds, that deepen, taking their toll. I long to share my struggles, to let my feelings flow, yet fear and judgment bind me, hiding what you don't know.

So when I seem distant or lost in my own mind, remember, dear children, my love for you is kind. It's not that I'm a child or choose to play a part, it's the ache of unspoken words that reside in my heart.

His Return

In a world so different from days of yore,
where miracles of old feel like folklore, how
would we know if he stood at our door, not
mistaken for a madman but Jesus once more?

No longer in robes and sandals adorned, but
perhaps in jeans and sneakers reborn.
His message of love is still timeless and true
yet disguised in a modern-day view.

Would we recognize his kindness and care
amid the chaos and noise everywhere?
In a sea of voices clamoring for attention, would
his words bring solace and comprehension?

If Jesus appeared in this fast-paced time, would
we see past the surface, past the grime?
To the heart that beats with compassion and grace,
seeing him not just in another unfamiliar face.

May we open our hearts and minds anew to
see the divine in each person we view.
For in every stranger, in every friend, his
spirit may dwell until the very end.

How Hard

In the quiet of the night, a solemn figure
stands, his heart heavy with knowledge
of fate's demanding hands.
Can we imagine the burden he carried with care,
knowing his loved one's destinies so heavy to bear?

With tender eyes that speak of love so deep,
he walks the path where sorrows steep.
The weight of the world upon his gentle soul
as he watches the story of time unfold.

His beloved apostles, dear to his heart, in their
future, he sees the pain they'll impart.
Yet he knows that this journey must be for
the greater purpose that all may see.

In the gardens of olives, he kneels and prays,
sweat-like drops of blood in the dark haze.
"Father, if it be your will," he quietly implores,
"let this cup pass from me." His heart was sore.

But then with resolve, he whispers,
"Not my will, but Thine," accepting the
path that was laid out in design.
For in his sacrifice, a greater love unfurled,
a gift of redemption for all the world.

So let us pause and ponder in awe, the depth of his
love without flaw. For in his sacrifice, a message
is clear that love conquers all, casting out fear.

Just a Friend

In silence, I often dwell, feeling the weight
of loneliness like a heavy spell.
But amid the darkness that surrounds, I
find solace in the faith that abounds.

Through tears and pain that never end, I
seek a human touch, a caring friend.
Though the days may be filled with sorrow, I
hold onto the hope for a brighter tomorrow.

God's presence is a comforting embrace, yet I
yearn for a human connection, a familiar face.
In this journey of solitude and strife, I long
for companionship to bring back life.

About the Author

Stephanie was adopted as a baby by an older couple and a natural daughter. There was emotional, physical, and mental abuse by her mother and adopted sister.

Stephanie was not told about God until she was almost a teen, but she believed that, in a way of his own, he let her know he was always there. And he has always been there for her through abuse, cancer, and dramatic life-changing health issues. Stephanie feels so blessed that God has been there for her, gifting her wonderful children and grandchildren. Stephanie knows her end is near, but it's all right because she knows God has a place for her with no more pain, where she will be able to walk again.